How to Make the Ideal, Repeatable Golf Swing

Table of Contents

Introduction 4

Chapter 1 5

   Keys to Good Golf 5

Chapter 2 12

   Making the Stroke 12

      The Forward Press and Reverse Press 12

         Raising the Club 14

         Review 14

         Hand Action 15

         Setting the Club 17

         Summary 21

Chapter 3 22

   Tips for Beginners 22

      Understanding Clubs 22

         Modern Clubs 23

         Clubs for Beginners 23

      Tips and Techniques for Approaching, Driving and Putting 23

         Driving 24

         Iron Shots 25

         Putting 25

         Avoiding hooking short putts 26

         Side hill putts 26

- Slicing and Hooking 27
- Side Hill Shots 28
- Up and down hill 28
- Special Trouble Spots 29
  - Shots into the wind 29
  - Sandtrap shots 30
  - Chip shots 30
- Conclusion 31

Introduction

The facts and fundamentals of any field do not change. This also remains true in the world of golf. Nevertheless, continued research and study have allowed new concepts to be cultivated and it is these concepts that have produced some rather precise conclusions which will be presented in the following pages.

It is quite regrettable that the thrills of this great game and even the recreational and health benefits which can be afforded by participation in this game are out of the reach of so many players simply because the game is so frequently misunderstood. For, while the game may be frequently misplayed, this is not due to any inabilities on the part of the player, but simply due to a lack of proper understanding of the game.

In reality, there is actually very little one needs to learn or know in order to play an excellent game of golf. Unfortunately, the lack of understanding regarding some key elements prevents many from enjoying the game.

Through a correct understanding of the facts of golf, the game can truly be enjoyable and can even be easy. To gain an understanding in how to improve your game, the following facts must first be established.

A golf club can and will only do what the player makes it do. The golf club on its own contains no special powers or abilities.

Each club is designed for a specific purpose. When and only when the club is applied to the ball in its natural state will the club produce the effect for which it was originally designed.

In this eBook, you will learn the many different ways you can begin to improve your golf game and achieve success with it. By establishing a plan, you will then be able to act aggressively and positively toward correcting errant tendencies while recognizing your errors. Through recognizing these errors you will be able to avoid them and then literally teach yourself how to play good golf, resulting in a natural sense of confidence.

Chapter 1

Keys to Good Golf

Far too frequently many golfers become so caught up in the essence of making the perfect shot that they fail to consider the basic keys to making a good shot. There are three essentials to any good golf game. Without mastering each of these three key elements it is impossible to achieve any level of success with your game.

Unfortunately, many players labor under the assumption that once they have mastered the ability to swing the club correctly the game should just naturally fall into place for them. This is highly incorrect. It must be stressed that each of the three key elements must be mastered in order for swings to be produced accurately and successfully.

The basic ability to swing the club correctly is certainly important. No successful game of golf can exist without it. That said; however, the only true correct way to swing the club is with a sense of body control. The ability to swing the club with body control is impossible; however unless a player also has the proper footwork to go along with it. If a player has not obtained a proper sense of balance so that he or she has full, unrestricted use of his body it will be impossible to obtain a correct swing. It is from the body that the power which generates the swing flows. Therefore, much of the success of the golf shot and the distance you can achieve, depends on how you use your body.

Second, players must be able to keep their club in the correct position so that it will produce the effect for which the club was designed. If this is accomplished, it will allow the ball to fly straight toward the goal without deviating. If you have noticed that your balls are not flying straight and true straight down the middle; if they are deviating left or right or anywhere other than the goal, the problem is most likely due to an inability to maintain the club in the correct position. This is where the importance of the grip comes in.

Finally, there is the matter of footwork. A player may be able to master his grip and a sense of body control; however, a lack of footwork can also spell disaster for any golf game.

When analyzing your golf game to determine where there is room for improvement, it is important to consider the following factors:

How well do you handle your weight? What is your sense of balance? Do you know how to work your feet and legs in order to set up the proper sense of balance so that your body can then be established as the motivating reason in swinging the club?

How well do you use your body? Can you feel there is a double-handed, ambidextrous motion in a golf swing in which an upswing as well as a downswing exists? Are you using your body in a way so that the upswing is made with the right side of the body while the downswing and follow through is established with the left side of the body?

Are you able to use your hands in order to exert the positioning control necessary over the club so that you can make the ball do precisely what you want it to do?

Individually, each of these aspects is certainly important and necessary. Beyond that; however, there is also a certain order of importance in order to establish a performance that will prevail in creating the ideal result for your game. For example, even if a golfer is using his body correctly in swinging the club, he must able know how to handle his body weight and only when he has established a working relationship between his body and his weight will be able to properly use his hands.

While this may sound somewhat complex, it can be explained simply. It is all a matter of timing.

First, one must learn to handle his or her weight. Simply shifting the weight from one foot to the other; however, will accomplish nothing on its own. This only places you in a position to where you can then utilize your body correctly.

Only when you have the basic footwork so that you are in a position in order to use your body to swing the club are your hands then free to exert the proper sense of control and position over the club. Quite simply, the shot will only fly as the club makes it fly and the flight of that ball is a direct result of the position of the club. The position of the club is directly linked to what your hands are doing and what your hands are doing is the factor that will determine the ultimate efficiency of your swing.

The three basic factors in any successful game of golf are:

- Footwork to achieve balance
- Body action to render power
- Hand action to maintain club control

The main problem for some golfers; however, is that they fail to obtain timing with these three factors. To be certain, the timing issue is delicate. Properly coordinating these three factors into an arrangement that works is a technique which requires attention.

A certain order of performance must be established so that the three basic operations of a golf swing can be properly executed. When properly combined and timed, the golfer is able to move smoothly from one maneuver to the next with all operations functioning collectively towards the final target of applying the club to the ball in a successful swing.

As Bobby Jones, the renowned golfer once stated, "My golf swing is a something that starts within me." It is certainly an accurate expression that the golf swing begins within the player. It is not something that is done with the club; instead it is something that is accomplished with the body.

In every stroke a golfer makes there are actually two swings as we discussed previously; the upswing and the downswing.

In order to accomplish the upswing the player must use the right side of his body by balancing with his weight on the right foot.

For the downswing to be executed, the player must use the left side of his body by balancing on his left foot.

An essential element in mastering the game lies in understanding that you cannot use your body any better than you can transfer your weight to the right foot so that the upswing can be accomplished with the right side of the body. Subsequently, you must be able to shift your weight to the left foot so that the downswing is accomplished on the left side. Therefore, it is critical that one learns to handle his weight so that the correct sides of the body can be used to accomplish the appropriate swings.

Once you have learned to re-shift your weight to the left foot so that the left side can be utilized in order to pull the club down and through the ball you will then be in a position to learn how to position your hands correctly.

You may note that as you swing the club up and down, there is a definite need to keep the club in the proper position as it is being swung up and down. This is accomplished with the hands; however, your hands will never be able to perform this critical function unless you have first established the ability to utilize your body as a way to motivate the club.

The importance of timing arises once again.

In a nutshell, this is really what the golf swing is all about. As we know, there are really only two basic requirements to every golf shot; distance and direction. Likewise, there are really only two things that you must learn in order to play a good game of golf; a sense of body control and body action in order to swing and stimulate the club and the proper way to achieve the action of the hands necessary to achieve the position of the club in order to regulate and determine the direction of the golf shot.

Every good golf player has the ability to produce different effects on the ball. One can make the golf ball go straight, slice or hook through a fairly simple manner.

For example, by turning the golf club in towards you (known as a closed position) you can use it to pull the ball to the left or curve it. You can also curve the ball to the right by simply positioning the club so that it is turned out away from you.

By keeping the club square, at an absolutely right angle to the line of the shot, the ball will fly completely straight.

The matter of obtaining a good golf swing therefore is really just a simple matter of training yourself to use your body to swing the club and then assuring your hands are free to exert the proper position control over the club so that it will fly true.

Assuming the correct position to the ball is the first half of any golf shot. The basic elements for assuming the correct position to the ball include:

- Assuring proper placement of the club to the ball
- Assuring correct hand positions or grip on the club
- Assuming correct placement of the feet
- Assuring proper positioning of the body

The four distinct moves to establishing the correct position to the ball can be accomplished in a step by step procedure that is quite simple.

Step 1: Place the club behind the ball by using only the left hand

While it is quite natural for the player to place the club behind the ball, a peculiarity in the construction of golf clubs could present a problem if you are not careful. The part of the club that meets the ball, the face, is not parallel with the shaft. Instead, it is hooked in. In other words, it is angled so that it will point off to the left a matter of a few degrees. If you are not familiar with this, problems can be established in this early step. By understanding the construction of the golf club you can then place the club properly to the ball. The proper way to place the club to the ball is to slant the handle of the club ever so slightly in the direction of the shot. By doing so, the left hand will then be positioned directly over the ball rather than over the club head. This slight change will allow you to:

- Create the position of the club during the swing
- Keep the club in the desired position
- Bring the club into and through the ball

Once the proper position of the left hand on the club has been assumed, the hand will rest more or less on top of the shaft. Three knuckles of the left hand will remain in clear view if you are looking down at your hand while the left thumb will be at a point that is somewhat behind the shaft.

This will happen quite naturally if the shaft of the club has been tilted forward slightly when it is positioned to the ball.

Step 2: Position the feet into place

The correct position to stand is in a place where the ball will be opposite to the left heel. Imagine a line which runs from the ball to the inside portion of the left heel. This will be at right angles to the line of the shot. Your feet must be placed so that the toes of both feet are parallel to the line of the shot. Keep in mind that this position should be assumed regardless of shot or club that is used. There is no need to change position when you change clubs. This will allow you to position the weight on your right foot so that you can use the right side of your body when raising the club to the top of the swing to make the stroke. As you bring the club down into and through the ball; you will be in a better position to shift your weight to the left foot and therefore use the left side of your body.

Make certain that your feet are never wider apart than the width of your shoulders. A narrow rather than a wide stance is always preferable because it allows you to shift your weight far easier.

Step 3: Bring the right hand to the club to complete the grip

Before this point your right arm should have remained inactive and should have been hanging rather naturally by your right side. Now is the time to bring the right hand to the club. You may note that when you bring the right hand to the club, with the club opposite to the left foot, you will need to relax the right knee somewhat.

Your right hand will assume a position on the club that is directly opposite to the position of the left hand. While the left hand lies on the top of the club handle, the right hand will assume a position that is somewhat underneath the club.

Many beginning players make the mistake of placing both hands directly on top of the club. If both hands are resting on top of the club, a one-handed effect is produced. As we discussed earlier, the correct position should be ambidextrous. The left hand should take care of the top of the club while the right hand takes care of the bottom of the club. Always remember that golf is a two-handed game.

When your hands are directly opposed to one another, both sides of the club will be under control and the club will rest in a pull and push action that is natural. This is the only action that will produce the desired leverage on the club.

Furthermore, it is imperative to check your grip and be sure that there is no tenseness in it. Any holding of the club should be confined to the first two fingers and thumb of each hand. Avoid using your entire fist to grip the club. In fact, the little finger of the right hand should not even touch the club.

Step 4: Turn the right heel out slightly

Most people naturally stand in a position in which both toes are turned out slightly. Therefore, it is important to make a conscious effort to turn the right heel out somewhat. This outward placing of the right heel will position the right foot in a far stronger position for the backswing. Additionally, it will also be far easier to shift the weight to your right foot when necessary.

Now, we have the sequence of moves that are necessary to get ready to play a golf shot:

Step 1: Place the club to the ball only using the left hand

Step 2: Place your feet into the correct position

Step 3: Relax the right knee to complete the grip

Step 4: Turn out the right heel slightly

The above steps will produce a natural sequence of moves where your weight, hands and body will be perfectly coordinated to line up. The more frequently this sequence of events is practiced, the more automatic it will become so that in a very short time the starting position will also be established automatically.

Chapter 2

Making the Stroke

The Forward Press and Reverse Press

After you have established the starting position, it is time to move on to the next part of the golf shot. This is the actual stroke or the actual swing of the club. If you have followed the moves described in Chapter 1, you should find this position will provide you with a sense of aim in order to feel the contact with the ball.

The next moves will place you in position where you will be able to lean the club against the ball. In order to do that; however, before you make any attempt to take the club away from the ball, you must shift your weight. Up until this point, your weight will most likely have been on your left foot. It is critical to change your balance from your left foot to your right in order to raise the club freely. The most successful players begin by assuming a position in which they are balanced on their left foot as they address the ball.

The best players also make a subtle point of shifting their weight and moving their balance from their left foot to their right foot before any attempt is made to raise the club to the top of the swing.

That said; there is really only one way in which you can change your balance from one foot to the other.

This is accomplished by changing your knee positions.

To change knee positions one merely reverses the positions. For example, you would bend the left knee and as you do so the right knee will straighten and by reversing the knee positions the weight and balance will now be on the right foot. This maneuver of changing knee positions provides the balance you need for the next step.

As we have previously discussed, any good game of golf is a double-handed, ambidextrous movement. Both hands must be used and both sides of the body must be used. The right side of the body is utilized for the upswing while the left side of the body produces the downstroke and follow through. Therefore, it becomes quite clear the difficulties one can encounter if not properly balanced on the right foot for the upswing and the left foot for the downswing.

By learning to handle your balance and weight you will be better prepared to execute the type of motion and action that is required for the correct shot.

In many ways, the human body is built like a pair of scissors. The left foot and right hand are extensions of one another. As a result, they always work together. The same is true for the right foot and left hand. While you may not realize it at the time, when you stand on your right foot, you are automatically restriction any action of your left arm and hand. Likewise, if you place your weight on your left foot, you will automatically be inhibiting the action of your right arm and hand.

Unfortunately, many golfers take this natural muscular arrangement to understand that the best game of golf can be played with one's weight divided evenly between both feet.

This is a complete falsehood.

Dividing your weight evenly between your feet does nothing to improve your golf game. Doing so will actually lock you up and destroy any chance you might have of achieving a natural, easy swing.

A good game of golf can only be accomplished by shifting your weight from the left foot to the right foot with a zig-zag movement. The first movement in this two-step process is known as the forward press in which the forward bend of the right knee and the forward press of the hands places you in the perfect position to assume the second move; which is the reversal of knee positions. This is known as the reverse press.

While the forward press and the reverse press as they are frequently known are important, it is critical that one does not become so focused on the importance of these two steps that you over exaggerate them. If this should occur, instead of the weight being properly shifted to the right foot in the reverse press, the weight may instead return back to the left foot; which can make it quite difficult to proceed with any kind of accurate swing.

Once you have accomplished the forward press and the reverse press, you will be able to execute them with such skill and assurance that they will generally be unnoticeable.

Raising the Club

The next step in the process is to raise the club to the top of the swing. Since you have already accomplished the last step, you should find yourself balanced on your right foot with the club positioned in the right hand.

Now, with the weight on the right foot and with the club positioned under the control of the right hand, you should find it quite natural and easy to raise the club to the top of the swing.

The following action should begin in the right hip with the entire right side of the body from hip to shoulder drawn back. The right arm will be naturally contracted, which will raise the club to the top of the swing.

Be aware at this point that you should not attempt to keep the right elbow locked in tight and close to the body. Instead, allow it to fall free and natural as if you were throwing a ball.

The next step is a reverse action on the left side of the body. This action, like the preceding step, will originate on the left side o the body and involve the left hip, contracting the left arm, as you pull the club down and through the ball.

The contraction, first on the right side with the right arm, will raise the club on the upswing. The reverse contraction on the left side using the left arm will pull the club down into and through the ball; providing you with a controlled technique for swinging the club. These contractions combined with body action and control, form the basis for a natural and easy game of golf.

As desirable as it might be, there is really no short-cut from the steps just described which will produce efficient and successful results. The three operations of footwork, body and hands are essential to each and every golf shot and cannot be accomplished without going through the moves described.

Let us take a moment to review these steps before moving on to the next subject, which will train you to strike the ball even if your eyes are closed.

Review

To assume the correcting starting position:

- Place the club to the ball using only the left hand
- Assume the correct position with your feet

- Finalize the grip by bringing the right hand to the club
- Turn the right heel slightly outward

To make the swing:

- Make the forward press
- Make the reverse press
- Raise the club to the top of the swing
- Bring the club down into and through the ball

Hand Action

These steps will hopefully have outlined the importance of a definite method of establishing a uniform position from which to take your golf shot. An established procedure for shifting your weight so that the body can be utilized as a means for motivating the club on the upswing as well as the downswing and follow through can prove to be critical, as we have discussed.

While a clear understanding has hopefully been reached on the combination of body action and weight shift, it is now time to turn our attention to another matter.

As we previously discussed, the three key elements of any good game of golf are footwork, body action and hand action. We have spent some significant time discussing in detail the importance of body action and weight shift. The hands; however, play an equally important role in not only placing the club in the correct position but also in maintaining it throughout the entirety of the swing.

Prior to this it was necessary to discuss the importance of body position for only when a player has established his body for the motivating control of the swing is he free to execute the proper positional control over the club with his hands.

Unfortunately, the positioning of the hands has led to the downfall of what could have many great golfers. Many of the erroneous ideas which persist among novice golfers serve only as a detriment.

Let us examine a few:

Perhaps one of the most common ideas is the thought that one should hold the club tightly in the back of the left hand. The idea behind this is that it will not allow the club to move away. In reality; however, this is quite contrary.

In other cases, golfers may attempt to exercise no wrist action on the backswing until they have achieved an above the waist position. When we examine this, it really fails to make any sense. How would it be possible to play a short shot off the edge of the green if this were the case?

As we examined in a prior section, when you assume the correct position to make the shot you will find yourself first balanced on your left foot. While you are in this position it will be difficult to take the club to the top of the swing until you actually shift your weight to the right foot. Through practice, this shift in weight will become a natural one-two movement. It is this forward press and subsequent reverse press that forms the basis of all good golf swings.

In a likewise natural manner, from the end of the reverse press your hands must now go to work. Much like the way you would prepare if you were about to throw something, it is necessary to raise the club to the top of the swing in a free, full and controlled motion.

When movement begins on the right side of the body it is quite natural to contract the right arms, as we discovered in a previous section. Consequently an immediate upward, pickup action of the club occurs. While the club is actually picked up using the right hand, there is simultaneously an automatic resistance on the left hand.

This counteracts the pickup action of the right hand. This combined action of the hands results in the club immediately being flipped and rather cocked into the position for the shot. It is this pickup action on the part of the right hand and the simultaneous downward thrust on the part of the left hand which produces the very powerful one-two action all correct golf shots must maintain.

A natural pull and push action which continues up through the backswing is acquired. Due to the pickup action on the part of the right hand arm cocking the right arm, the leverage action is actually reversible. Thus, a powerful thrust can be applied on the downswing and follow through.

At the same time, the arm is placed into an extended position from which it can naturally produce a pull action on the downswing from the thrust of the left hand and arm in this cocking position of the club. In reality, it is this pull with the left and thrust with the right on the downswing that creates a powerful swing.

The pickup pull and downward push of the hands will flip the clubhead to a 45 degree angle. Within this angle area, the club becomes set for the shot. If the clubhead is moved beyond this 45 degree angle area, you can rest assured the hands are not balanced. If the hands are not working together in an even manner one or the other will be too strong during the swing. As a result the club will move out of position and the shot will go astray.

To prevent this, there would be a perceptible separation between your hands. Many times golfers attempt to resist this separation, resulting in disaster. The separation should remain constant on the backswing.

On the downswing the action of the hands will be reversed, with a contraction of both hands while they come together to create a strong formation as the ball is met. The first two fingers and thumb of the right hand create the upward pickup pull which you can feel. Likewise, the downward thrust is created with the left thumb and the knuckle at the base of the left forefinger on the left hand.

Avoid trying to create a downward thrust or a push with the heel of the left hand. Likewise, do not attempt to lock the back portion of the right hand. In either case you will not be able to achieve free movement of the club. All action is accomplished with the thumb and the first two fingers or the front or fore part of both hands.

This natural pull and push action of both hands will allow the power from the body to radiate to the club in a perfectly straight line. In reality, this is the only way in which force or power can be applied. This straight line will naturally blend with what your body is already doing during the swing, creating a perfect shot.

Setting the Club

Having mastered this push and pull action, it is important to understand that you can maintain control over what the ball does by properly setting it into one of three positions. These three positions into which the club can be cocked or set will produce three separate results.

1. You can curve the ball to the right-known as the fade or slice

2. You can curve the ball to the left-known as the pull or hook

3. You can drive the ball perfectly straight

Whether the ball hooks to the left, flies absolutely straight or slices to the right completely depends on the position of the club upon impact.

By using your hands at the outset of the backswing it is completely possible to cock or set the club into a certain position in which it will automatically be in the desired position upon impact. The position into which you set the club on the backswing will determine exactly what the position of the club will be at impact with the ball.

The three positions into which you can set the club are:

1. The open position. This position will produce a slice. The face of the club should be turned towards the sky while the shaft of the club should be tilted toward the outside of the line of flight; moved away from the right toe. Whenever you desire a high flying shot that will stop just short of landing, the open face technique should be used. A word of caution; however, if the position is too open it will resolve in a curve or slice to the right. You can also use the open position to play shots out of deep sand traps.

2. The closed position. This position will produce a hook. In this position the face of the club will turned towards the ground while the shaft will be tilted toward the inside of the line of flight toward the right toe. You can use the closed face technique for playing low shots that will run. Beware; however, that if the position is overly exaggerated, it will result in a curve to the left.

3. The square position, which will produce straight flying shots. In this position, the face3 of the club will be kept square to the line of the shot. Keep in mind, it is best to keep the shaft of the club tilted somewhat to the inside of the line of the shot in order to offset an inward pull of the left side as the club is brought through the ball.

As we previously learned, when you take a position to make a shot, you will find yourself balanced on your left foot. As a result it becomes necessary for you to shift your weight to the right foot by using a one-two movement; the forward press and then the reverse press.

Through these two movements the weight will be shifted to the right foot, you will be set to raise the club to the top of the swing using your right side and at that very moment your hands must be ready to set the club into the desired position to create the desired outcome.

As your right hand applies the sharp pickup action to the club, the left hand must simultaneously be able to perform its own crucial action; that is the setting of the club into the desired position.

It is extremely important to note that it is actually the left hand that will determine exactly how the club will be set.

You see, if the left hand turns inward toward the body, a plan can move the club to an open position. This pronating movement will allow the face of the club to be moved toward the sky while at the same time tilting the club shaft to the outside of the line of flight. This combination of movements will produce slices and high flying shots.

If; however, the left hand is turned away from the body, then quite naturally the club face will subsequently be closed and turn towards the ground. Simultaneously, through this supinating movement, the club shaft will be tilted to the inside of the line of flight towards the right shoe. As a result, you will be able to produce shots that run, fly low and hooks.

If your left hand moves toward a middle course and neither supinates or pronates then the club face will be automatically squared to the line of flight and you will be able to produce straight flying shots.

Notice that throughout all of these three different positions, both hands remain active. The action of the right hand; however, remains the same throughout each of the three different positions; a sharp pickup action of the club. It is action of the land which differentiates in each position. A pronation can occur; a downward thrust through an inward move or a supination may result; an outward move. One may also produce a straight in-between position.

Therefore, the key to understanding and producing consistent results lies in an awareness of what the left hand is doing. This failure to understand and properly utilize the land hand is what often makes golf such a difficult game for many. Your left hand can work no better than your right hand will allow. While the process of setting the club into position is most definitely a two-handed action; which originates with the right hand; the final result actually depends on the left hand.

The final finesse of being able to make the ball fly low or high, make it run or stop or make it slice or hook is entirely dependent on the club position. That critical club position is entirely dependent on the action of the left hand. Without proper body action and footwork it is impossible; however, to keep the hands working in the right position.

The crux of the final shot may lie in the positioning of the left hand; however, as we have come to learn the left hand cannot achieve the correct position without the golfer achieving the correct combination of efforts using the feet, body and hands together.

You may have noticed that some golfers like to go through a series of ritualistic movements before they actually go into their swing. In some cases, these movements can even be somewhat amusing. Some golfers even exhibit movements which are so exaggerated prior to their swing that they become a distraction to both their partners and their opponents. As disturbing as these actions can be; there is generally one clear purpose for them.

They are an attempt for the golfer to find a proper sense of balance.

If you watch professional golf you will note that even professional golfers will assume a position to the ball, do a forward press, a reverse press, cock the club to the 45 degree angle and then return to their original position and repeat the entire process all over again before they finally sail off into a smooth swing.

By no means should it be necessary to wiggle and waggle to the point that you are not only a distraction to others but you also slow down play on the entire course. That said; however, it is impossible for a golfer to go into a swing unless he is right on his feet with the club in the correct position. There will be absolutely no point in swinging the club if it is not in the correct position. To do so is to court disaster.

If professional golfers cannot play well without insuring they have achieved the right balance and club position prior to making the swing, how would it be possible for a regular player to achieve any degree of success if he overlooks these important initial maneuvers?

It is absolutely imperative for any golfer hoping to achieve success to establish his balance and know how to move the club into the right position before the swing is actually made.

Constant repetition of these actions will provide you with an instinctive ability to perform them without even thinking about it.

Summary

By practicing the necessary sequence of action it is possible to learn to produce swings which are consistent and which routinely result in the desired outcome each and every time. It is important; however, to ensure that you do not deviate from the required sequence of action.

First, learn how to handle your weight in order that you can use it to motivate the club. Without this necessary action your hands will not be free and ready to fall into line. Once your hands are free and ready, they will naturally work together to set and maintain the club in line.

Through routine and consistent practice, you will gain the ability to cock the club into position at the beginning of the backswing. You will find that your hands will become so interrelated to their own job that in reality the only way to swing the club will be to do so with your body. This is really the only kind of golf swing which can be delicate or powerful, as needed in order to produce entirely consistent results.

Chapter 3

Tips for Beginners

Understanding Clubs

As we have discussed throughout prior sections, with proper practice and understanding of key elements, golf is an easy game to play. This is true because the club actually does the work. When golf clubs were first introduced there were only four clubs. They were:

1. The driver-used for the long distance shots from the tee

2. The brassie-a protective brass plate covered the bottom of the club to use for distance shots from the fairway

3. The baffie-a club with quite a bit of loft on the face so that it would raise the ball high into the air. This club was used for approach shots to the green

4. The putter-a club designed to roll the ball on the ground and into the cup

Interestingly, these first golf clubs were all made of wood and looked somewhat like a hockey stick. As the game of golf developed and evolved over the years, the idea of a splice model club with a head and shaft glued together at an angle and joined together with a strong waxed cord was conceived of.

Further innovations resulted in a myriad of developments of the golf club. Over the years three different types of clubs have developed; drivers, putters and irons. These three types of clubs actually represent the three different areas of golf. Nevertheless, for quite some time golfers went to extreme lengths in preparing for their games. In some instances, it was noted that golfers were bringing as many as two dozen different golf clubs with them out onto the course. The United States Golf Association, which felt that this wide array of equipment could possibly discourage those who were interested in taking up the game, passed a rule that a player could not have more than 14 clubs in his golf bag. That remains the rule today.

Modern Clubs

Today, a standard set of clubs consists of four drivers, which are numbered 1-4; eight irons numbered 2-9; a heavy weight club known as the sand wedge and a putter. Basically the only difference between the four woods is the degree of loft on the face of the club; which will tend to elevate the ball on a higher angle of trajectory.

This is also true of the irons. Each iron will introduce a somewhat different angle of trajectory.

As a result each driver in a set of woods and a set of irons are designed to produce a certain angle of flight. This serves to emphasize the important fact that clubs do not actually produce the effect for which they were designed unless they are all swung and applied to the ball in the same manner.

When a golfer uses the same swing on all of his clubs the game can be quite easy.

Clubs for Beginners

If you are a beginner to the game of golf you can obtain golf clubs which are uniform in terms of grip, weight, balance and shaft tension. These clubs are made available in various price ranges and are also available in sets consisting of number which are less than the maximum of 14 permitted by the rules.

Ideally, it is best to avoid clubs which are too heavy. Likewise, it is important to avoid clubs with shafts which seem to be too stiff. The ideal balanced club is a D2 swing shaft with a shaft of medium tension.

The same is not true for women golfers; however. The average woman golfer would do far better with a C7 with the shaft having a flex tension.

An abbreviated set will allow even beginners to operate quite capably. This set would consist of two drivers; usually a #2 and #4 wood. Four irons would also be included; typically #3, 5, 7, 9, a sand wedge and a putter. This half set of clubs will provide a nice complete range of shots. If one wishes, one can add the clubs which have been omitted from the set at a later time.

Tips and Techniques for Approaching, Driving and Putting

As you may have noted, the ideas behind the tips presented thus far have been to establish that the swing is the element which will produce consistent results in every shot. The technique and the procedure should remain the same in every shot with the goal established as propelling the ball to a certain spot.

The golfer must be able to control two things in order to accomplish this goal:

1. He must be able to control the direction of the shot

2. He must be able to control the distance it travels

As we have previously discussed, the only way to accomplish this is through practice. It is imperative that the form be practiced until the swing can be expanded to provide the power along with the drive necessary to achieve the goal. Once this has been accomplished, it is necessary to continue practicing until the form has been finely honed to the delicate touch which is required to achieve the desired outcome while actually on the green.

While nothing can be substituted for practice; a few suggestion and tips can assist in the development of various shots.

Driving

Distance may always be required on tee shots; however, it is necessary to train yourself not to press. Keep in mind that the additional length of the shaft will automatically develop additional power through the increased leverage provided by the extra length. You will need additional time for the extra length of the driver to reach the top of the swing as well as to get back to the ball. To compensate for this, you will need to develop a somewhat languid sort of rhythm when using your driver.

Using the #2 driver for your tee shots can help you gain the practice you need for this rhythm. The added loft on the #2 will help to absorb any slight errors that can occur from mistiming that might occur if you are using your #1 driver.

The more lofted drivers should ideally be used first by beginners. You can move on to using the less lofted clubs as your swing improves.

It is also important to take care not to grip the club too tightly when you are striving for distance. This will only serve to destroy the required hand action. In addition, avoid spreading your feet and staking too wide a stance. Doing so will obliterate your footwork and as we now know, without footwork there can be no balance and consequently no power.

Iron Shots

Once again, the importance of 'do not press' must be stressed. Take care to select eh club which will obtain the distance required. When playing your irons, it is imperative to make an effort to coast along just as much as needed without forcing the shot. This will provide you with the reserve necessary when the situation calls for it. Make an effort to adopt a narrow stance which will permit an easy shift of weight. Ultimately this will allow the body to be used for the power required for your shots.

Putting

Of course, the real objective of the game of golf is to get the ball into the cup. One can drive well and even approach well and as important as these two elements are to the game, they are nothing if one cannot get the ball into its desired destination.

A number of different methods can provide the power necessary to achieve a putting stroke; however, that does not mean that all of them are equally effective. The best style capable of producing the power necessary emanates from the body. After you have learned to use your body correctly, your hands will naturally fall into a line which will provide you with a natural direction to guide and control the club. This combination of using the body for power along with the hands for control will produce drives which are long and straight as well as accurate iron shots and resounding fairway woods.

Let us stop and examine this for a moment. If you are able to achieve control and accuracy with the technique at a range of 200 or more yards, does it not make sense that this same technique will provide even more control and greater accuracy at a range that is ten feet or less?

The same requirements of direction and distance are necessary on every putt. If you are able to achieve that with same control on long shots, then it only makes sense that you should be able to apply the same technique and style to your short shots.

In reality, the objecting in putting is the exact same objective in any other shot. That is distance plus direction.

Perhaps the most important key to putting is the ability to gauge the speed of the green. Generally a putt will not be driven off the line. Most frequently trouble arises when the putt falls short by six feet and then the golfer is forced to overshoot the cup by a few feet on the next stroke.

If you use the routine which we have previous established, this should not occur as it established the body control necessary to achieve the putting stroke.

Before moving on, it is important to note that in order to avoid any tension in the hands which would destroy this necessary control it is important to make sure your little finger is not resting on the club. This was pointed out earlier, however, we will go into it in more detail here.

The smallest finger should never be resting on the club. This creates too much tension. Instead, take the little finger off the club and curl it under. This position will bring the hands close together and form a leverage action that will produce the desired body action.

Avoiding hooking short putts

In most instances when a short putt is missed it winds up on the left side of the cup. This is because the player is invariably holding his body still. As the hands move past the body there is a natural tendency for the hands to turn and actually roll the putter to the left.

In order to combat this problem, it is necessary to learn to pull the club across the line of the putt from the outside inward. One must draw the club across the ball as if you are attempting to produce a slice; effectively cutting across the ball. This will actually keep the putter square to the line of the shot. Begin by applying this to short two foot putts and then gradually apply it on longer puts. You will be surprised at how square the putter blade will remain.

Side hill putts

Keep in mind on side hill putts that the ball will travel straight for the first portion of the putt and then drift on the slope as the speed of the ball begins to die down. It is important to discern at which point the ball will begin to break and then aim for that point and allow the ball to float inward from that point. By learning to putt for that breaking point you can see a tremendous improvement.

Slicing and Hooking

While slicing and hooking would seem to be completely opposite from one another, it is important to point out that only when a player is able to fully understand both extremes is he able to consistently play down the middle of the fairway. It is only through this understanding that he will know what to avoid in order to achieve the desired outcome.

As we all know, each golf course contains its own hazards. Whether that is trees, bunkers or sandraps, they exist and regardless of how well one plays a golfer is bound to find himself in one difficulty or another at some time.

When this situation occurs the proper selection of the correct club can help to solve the problem. For example, one can produce a very low flying shot with a #2 iron or a driver. Likewise, one can produce a very high shot with a #9 iron.

There are some situations; however, in which the ball should be deliberately curved to the right or even brought around to the left. This can be rather easily accomplished if the player has taken the time to develop the most basic form.

Once again it must be stressed that the game of golf can be relatively simply if one accepts the fact that all one must do is simply swing the club. The club itself will do the work. The driver will drive the ball. The iron will lift the ball. The putter will roll the ball.

In every single shot, beginning with the driver and extending all the way to the putter, the same movement that we established early from the starting position to the swing is necessary. The simplicity lies in applying the form to an extended degree for long shots and then merely reducing it for short shots.

If you apply this pattern of movement on every shot you will notice that your movements become motivated to produce directional control. This control will then be regulated by the manner in which you set your club at the outset. The only factor that you must concentrate on is how much power you are going to generate with your body action.

Due to the fact that two swings exist, the upswing and the downswing, it is necessary for an underlying weight shift to exist so that the action of the body can be properly delivered. While no short cut exists for this technique, it is a relatively simple three point execution.

In every shot, from drive to putt, there must exist:

1. Footwork to achieve balance

2. Hand action for club position

3. Body action for power

The object, of course, throughout the game is to drive the ball. Balancing these three factors will help you learn how to control power when necessary rather than allowing it to dissipate and ruin your shots.

Side Hill Shots

When playing from a position on a side hill, your foot position will naturally be lower than the spot where the ball lies. Because of this there will exist a tendency for a very flat swing. As a result, a hook shot will inevitably occur. In some cases, it may be practical to use a hook shot. If that is the case then it should by all means be used and the shot played naturally. If a hooked shot would place you into a troubled position; however, then it will be necessary to offset the hook by setting your club into an open position. The final result be a straight shot rather than a slice or a hook.

If you find yourself standing on ground that is higher than the ball, there will generally exist a tendency to slice. Once again, if you find it practically to slice, then do so. If; however, that would present problems then you can offset the effect of the slice by cocking your club into a closed position. A straight shot will once again be produced.

You may find it necessary in such side hill shots to use a stronger club. This will allow you to use a shorter swing without the possibility of losing your balance and possibly missing the shot all together.

Up and down hill

In the event the ball is lying on a downhill lie, it can be helpful to avoid playing the ball directly opposite the left heel. Instead, take a stance where the ball is positioned opposite a point that is nearer the center of the body.

When you play the ball back you will create an automatic technique of contracting the ball on the downswing. This will force the ball to climb more in its flight.

Interestingly, the same method can be used during hill lies. The reason for this is that from this position it is difficult to re-shift the weight back to the left foot.

Special Trouble Spots

A wide variety of trouble shots can all quite easily and capably be handled with one simple remedy. As we previously discussed, the ball should be played at a point that is opposite the inside part of the left heel in all shots.

You may recall that the reason for this is that on the backswing the weight would be shifted to the right foot. In order for the player to make the downswing and the follow through; however, the weight would need to be shifted to the left foot. When impact occurs the weight is on the left foot and as a result the swing will center opposite from that point.

When playing difficult shots; however, it is necessary to actually lower the contact point. You can accomplish this by moving the ball back somewhat. You will then be playing at a point that is opposite the right heel as the situation calls for it. To put it another way, the deeper the ball is implanted, the further back the opposite right heel must be positioned; with the club resting in a somewhat closed position.

As a result, of course, the further back it is played the more lofted the club must be. This is the only time when there is an exception to the standard rule that the ball must be played opposite the left heel.

When you find yourself in such a trouble spot, play nearer the right foot and you will be surprised by how easy it will be to achieve a swing that will motivate the ball out of deep grass or even out of a cuppy lie.

Shots into the wind

When facing a shot into the wind, if you utilize a straight faced iron in the same manner just described, back off the right foot, you will be able to produce a shot that is long and powerful. This technique is often referred to as a push shot and new golfers are frequently apprehensive about attempting it. If you find yourself topping the ball or unable to pick it up on the fairway lies; however, simply moving the ball back towards your right heel will generally put an end to those problems.

Sandtrap shots

In the event the ball is not buried in the sand and it is not necessary to lift the ball sharply, the method just described can be quite reliable. When you play the ball back opposite the right foot, you can make clean contact with the ball and cause it to actually be on its way before the club even encounters the sand. Try it and you will find there is no other reliable and consistent way to get out of a sandtrap.

If; however, you find it necessary to raise the ball quickly, then you will need to play the ball opposite the left heel with the club in an open position rather than opposite the right heel in a closed position. Take care to keep the club in the open position throughout the swing.

This technique will provide you with the ability to move the ball out of the sand and land it on the green with very little difficulty at all.

Chip shots

It becomes quite essential to play the ball back opposite the right hell on the short shots that exist just off the edge of the green. This technique will insure you are able to get beneath the ball properly and avoid contacting the ball with the edge of the club; thereby skating it across the green in a haphazard manner.

For better chip shots; however, it is important to understand one key factor.

It is the body action which provides the power while the hands are free to control the direction or halt the effect from an open face club position. Once again, the importance of how the club is set for the shot is established.

When playing a chip shot, the player may use a lofted club, such as a #9 iron, in order to automatically place a halt on the ball. One may also use a #4 or even a #3 iron to put a roll on the ball in a likewise manner. That said; however, there is definitely a degree of added control that can be achieved with all of these shots if the player has practiced the action of playing the club open when it is necessary to achieve a sharp stop on a chip shot. Likewise, if the goal is to achieve a roll or run shot, you can more easily accomplish this with the ability to set the club into a closed position as you play the shot.

Of course, practically speaking, the best way to play a chip shot is to always play them with a closed face position of the club. By using a club that will drop the ball onto the smooth putting surface, you can then have it roll or run on up to the cup.

Playing the ball off the right foot instead of opposite the left heel can help to facilitate this pitch and run effect.

Conclusion

When all is said and done, the game of golf is a completely natural and easy game to play. Sadly; however, many people simply make the game difficult to learn by failing to understand the procedures that should be used. The inability to succeed in golf most frequently arises from a lack of understanding rather than a lack of physical ability in the player. This certainly can explain why individuals who have achieved great success in a variety of other sports fail to perform well on the golf course.

The tendency to create problems on the golf course is a problem which is sadly widespread. The very nature of golf requires an understanding on the part of the player and unlike many other games that are played with a ball the player must attain an instinctive ability to get into the right position for play. Golf is no different.

A definite plan of action and style must be established. While the position of the ball does not always lend itself to a nice setting, by training oneself to act routinely, a player can compensate for this. A definite plan to begin and complete each shot consistently will result in none other than consistent results.

Rather than rushing into a game of golf, developing an understanding of what to do, how to do it and practicing that plan until it becomes routine, will help any player to develop the confidence which is so essential to good performance on the golf course.

www.ingramcontent.com/pod-product-compliance
Lightning Source LLC
LaVergne TN
LVHW020742090526
838202LV00057BA/6180

9 783986 085421